Why Cats Do That

© 2001 Karen Anderson
Illustrations © Wendy Christensen

Published by Willow Creek Press, P.O. Box 147, Minocqua, Wisconsin 54548

Design by Pat Linder
Edited by Andrea Donner

Library of Congress Cataloging-in-Publication Data
Anderson, Karen, 1958–
Why cats do that : a collection of curious kitty quirks / by Karen Anderson ; illustrations by Wendy Christensen.
p. cm.
ISBN 1-57223-405-9 (hardcover : alk. paper)
1. Cats—Behavior—Miscellanea. I. Christensen, Wendy. II. Title.
SF446.5 .A529 2001
636.8'0887--dc21
2001003687

Printed in Canada

Why Cats Do That

A Collection of Curious Kitty Quirks

by Karen Anderson

Illustrated by Wendy Christensen

Willow Creek® PRESS

MINOCQUA, WISCONSIN

Thanks to the following models whose likenesses appear in these pages:

Petunia

Princess Dagny

Lady GreyShadows

Bunny

Tiger

Gretel

Dandelion

Dominique

Sir Sterling Silver Longfellow

Handsome Harry, Wizard of Bobcat Mountain

Ada Augusta Abigail Tabitha

Chrysanthemum

Pearl

For Buttons and Daisy Mae

— K.A.

*Dedicated to Petunia, Queen of the
Calicos, for over nineteen years my
muse, companion, model, advisor,
mentor, teacher and friend.*

— W.C.

Contents

Preface

Cats are like curious art objects come to life, and watching them go about their daily routine is sometimes like following around an art show. You're not sure what you'll see next, but you know it's going to be good. You plan on being captivated, entertained, enlightened, moved, astounded, possibly a bit disturbed and yes, even puzzled. These are some of the rewards of living with the enigmatic feline and this is the reason this book was written.

It is my belief that the cat is one of the most fascinating, graceful and beautiful creatures on the earth, and thus makes a wonderful subject to gaze upon and to study.

Part of the fun and challenge of being around cats is figuring out their sublime, even strange, ways of expressing things such as contentment, anxiety, affection, curiosity or anger. The fact that cats have retained so much of their wildness and so many of their strong, ancient feline instincts further invites long and loving observation. As with any animal, cats do peculiar things for their own reasons; the mystery that surrounds cats is particularly legendary.

Cat body language is covered in some detail here to take a bit of the guesswork out of determining your cat's true state of mind and heart; body language won't ever stop working and it cannot tell a lie.

A docile-looking cat may appear happy, but certain whisker, ear and tail positions might announce just the opposite. Wouldn't you like to discover what it all means? You can learn what your cat's body is revealing, and you'll be pleasantly surprised by the mutual enjoyment your efforts at deciphering will bring. It can only enrich the friendship you have with your cat.

Why Cats Do That is intended to embellish your general understanding of every domestic cat that treads the earth and to motivate you to thoroughly explore the beguiling ways of your own *felis catus*. Take the time to study, to photograph, to draw or paint these resplendent creatures. Indeed, may the cats in your life keep you quietly *oohing* and *aahing* for years to come.

Why do cats rub against everything in sight?

At the core of the answer to this question lies one of the most appealing characteristics of the feline. When a cat rubs against the corner of a sofa, the arm of a chair, a shoe in the hallway, or especially some part of a person, it is purposefully choosing the thing as its own. "This is mine more than it is yours" the ultra-territorial cat is announcing, and don't you forget it.

Whether cats are outdoors marking trees, steps, fences and benches, or indoors claiming furniture, walls, and people, they are very intentionally depositing their individual feline scent by way of special glands on the fore-head, around the mouth, under the chin, near the ears, and even between the toes.

One rub is hardly enough though, as cats must continually refresh each spot they have visited to declare their rights to the next cat who comes along.

Depending upon how many other cats step into his territory, a site might be frequented and marked several times per day.

When your cat comes alongside and tenderly nudges you, he's not only un-abashedly declaring to the world that he considers you his property, he is also showing you genuine affection and a sincere desire for physical contact. As the cat lovingly slides its tail or chin along your leg, arm, or face with per-haps a slight pause and a purr, the unique scent he leaves behind is min-gled with your unique scent (both undetected by our noses) which then produces a new "twosome" scent, something the cat finds great pleasure in creating over and over again.

Daily, incessantly, sometimes even forcefully and maybe not so quietly, the cat bonds with us, aligns with us, and attaches himself to us.

Why do cats scratch the furniture?

Cats view our furniture as truly the most divine scratching apparatus that could be conceived of, and they must be entirely confused when we dissuade them from using it for the obvious intended purpose! There sits the wicker love seat, the upholstered chair and that nice big sofa, just waiting for kitty to sharpen her claws at whim.

Actually, cats aren't technically sharpening their claws as they scratch but are instead stripping away the old, dull claw sheaths to expose brand new sharp claws beneath. This is a powerful feline instinct that drives the cat to keep its claws in top form at all times. While kitty is vigorously scratching, her claws are also getting practice extending and retracting, which is essential to catching prey, fighting, and climbing. The front legs and shoulders are getting stretched and strengthened too, depending on how fervently the cat is scratching.

And don't forget the ever-important scent marking! There are scent glands on the underside of the front paws which are madly secreting kitty's special mark.

Scratching can also be deployed as an attention-getting tool, simply because the cat has figured out that the sound of shredding furniture can easily get you to notice her. But don't dismay — with some gentle, consistent correction and the presence of a large, sturdy scratching post, you can probably save most of your furniture.

Why do cats like small spaces?

A cat can make quick work of disarraying even the tidiest linen closet or lingerie drawer. Cats are fond of closet shelves, drawers, baskets, boxes, and other hideaways because they feel snug and protected in smaller, defined places. The sides of a basket, the walls of a box (even a box lid) or a stack of pillows all provide a miniature fortress for kitty when she wants to slip away unnoticed or simply enjoy an undisturbed nap. (I think most of us can relate.)

A cat who is especially fearful or upset might be found under beds and sofas — the harder to reach, the better.

Kitty's love of cramped quarters is why cats don't mind cat carriers. From the cat's point of view, if the humans insist on hauling them to the dreaded vet and back, please let it be in a sturdy, secure carrying case. It is the unusual cat who prefers to roam the inside of a car and kitty usually ends up under the seat anyway.

Why do cats like high places?

High elevations are attractive to kitty because they're relatively safe and because the view is ever so much better from several feet in the air! Whether it's overlooking the backyard or the living room, the feline must, must, must regularly monitor her territory — the higher the perch the better. Unless deep into sleep, the cat doesn't want to miss a thing. She logs all the comings and goings of house-mates, her human companions, prey and potential enemy. Trees, fences, and rooftops outside the house and window sills, sofa backs, and entertainment centers inside the house are favorite watchtowers for cats.

Regardless, the whole idea is for kitty to check out absolutely everything from a secure site, high above danger. Of course no self-respecting cat would pass up the opportunity for a nice, peaceful elevated nap either. Who could blame them?

Why do cats sleep all day?

They don't! Well all right, they do clock around sixteen hours of sleep during every 24 hour period and they are a nocturnal animal, but it would be a stretch to say that cats sleep all day long. (Some cats sleep out of boredom, but that's the owner's fault, not kitty's.)

You've heard the term cat nap? Well, it didn't originate from us. The cat's sleep patterns hearken back to its ancestors' life on the savanna when not a single hunting opportunity could be missed. A cat quickly and skillfully stalks and kills its prey, and thus must be ready to respond to a fast-moving dinner morsel at any given moment. The feline body is suited for short, potent bursts of energy and has adapted a sleep style to accommodate. Cats usually sleep lightly and more often, in order to gain in length of sleep what they may lack in depth. The cat is far from lazy but instead has truly perfected the nap and mastered the art of pacing oneself throughout the day.

So the next time you pass by kitty all cozy and curled up, just remember that you are witnessing some highly efficient sleep management.

Why do cats' tails whop, wave and quiver?

The tail of a cat is beautiful and graceful, all the while silently conveying much of what a cat would say if it could speak in words. It curls and dips and swooshes. It whips and darts and sweeps. A cat's tail floats through the air behind him as he walks and wraps right around him like a scarf as he sits. Besides its role as a kitty barometer, the feline tail is also used for balance (especially along a ledge or fence). Decoding every tail message isn't always possible but there are a few tail positions we understand. A high flying tail is a good sign and usually means kitty is happy and secure in her surroundings. A tall quivering tail (from the base on up) is a sign that kitty is bursting with excitement or anticipation; a treat is about to land in her food bowl perhaps, or you have just walked through the doorway after being away. A whopping tail is either a sign of growing discontent (which may lead to anger) or a kind of

excited indecision. For instance, kitty might be lying somewhere looking comfortable and even enjoying a good petting session when all of a sudden her tail will start whopping up and down or back and forth. She could be getting annoyed with the petting or sensing that you're about to stop petting her. She may be deciding what to do next and has too many options. Cats also whop their tails when they notice prey, but do not (or can not) go after it. Vigorous whopping back and forth of the tail indicates that the cat is becoming quite irritated; her tail display could be warning of an attack. Most of the time, however, a whopping tail signals only moderate displeasure.

When the cat's tail slowly and very gently waves back and forth, she's happy, relaxed, and delighted with what's going on. You might be stroking her, conversing lovingly, about to present her with a treat or even playing gently. She could be responding to a meaningful massage, the

perfect scratch of her ears, or a great chin rub. Often the whole length of tail waves but kitty could also curl just the tip of her tail to speak pleasure. Sometimes a cat's tail will whop and wave simultaneously, indicating her feelings at the moment are quite complex. She's loving some things and not so sure about others — now doesn't that just about sum up the cat?

Why do cats spray?

This offensive behavior is perhaps the human equivalent to sending a forthright letter stating a very strong, conflicting opinion or even the posting of a large "Keep Off" sign on one's property. Cats don't have these options so they "shout" their announcements within the feline community by spraying urine in noticeable, significant spots.

Spraying is different from plain urinating in that the cat sprays vertical surfaces (such as a wall or a chair) rather than horizontal surfaces (like the ground). Also, the bladder isn't emptied and the spraying cat isn't about to cover up the scent afterward!

All cats have the ability to spray, whether male, female, un-neutered or neutered but it's the male cats who do it most often and with the most gusto. When a tomcat sprays he is either advertising his sexual availability to the female cats in the area or announcing to every cat in no uncertain terms that he considers the area to be his territory. Of course nothing is going to prevent another cat from stopping by to take issue with that pronouncement and spray their urine right over the other guys. And so it goes. Even a neutered male cat will spray as best he can when perturbed by a spraying tomcat who insists on trespassing and marking his domain.

Female cats sometimes spray to signal to the toms that they are in heat or if they feel crowded or threatened by another feline invader.

Why do cats shift their whiskers in and out?

Besides contributing to those famous feline good looks and perhaps reminding us of a mustache, the cat's whiskers are great mood indicators.

When a cat's whiskers are clumped together and pressed close to kitty's face, she is feeling extremely timid, shy or defensive. Conversely, when the whiskers are fanned out and spreading, the cat is tense for one reason or another — not necessarily nervous but certainly excited. This whisker display doesn't automatically indicate that kitty will attack, but it is the one cats use just before an aggressive move. Depending upon the circumstances, she could become threatening, but more than likely she is simply being her benevolent inquisitive self.

Some cats might also extend their whiskers as an ardent request for stroking and attention. The most common state-of-the-whiskers is full extension, out sideways, not spreading too far. Kitty is letting the world know that she's relaxed, comfortable, friendly, content, ambivalent, or even bored.

The cat reserves the right to hold plenty of mystery — and to be honest, we probably wouldn't have it any other way.

Why do cats rotate their ears?

Because they can. If we could manage to turn, lower, and flatten our ears I suppose we'd show them off, too. But we cannot and they can, so cats use their soft, stylish, symmetrical ears to speak nonverbally to us and to other cats. Not only do their ears house intricate canals and receptors that grant the cat truly amazing hearing, they're also able to tell us much about a cat's state of mind.

When a cat's ears are tall and pointed forward but slightly outward, kitty is content, aware, listening, and relaxed. Hopefully, this is how your cat looks most of the time. The ears could be facing different directions, depending upon where multiple sounds are coming from. (Try that yourself!)

When kitty's ears are facing straight ahead and totally erect, he's alert and focusing on a new sound; the cat is on guard and inclined to go investigate rather than curl up and relax.

Flattened ears mean the cat is frightened. Cats do this with each other when they are involved in a stand-off; when the ears go down like this, it means something is about to happen. The cat could be seconds away from an all-out attack or frightened enough to look for an escape route and run. Either way, kitty is pulling her ears down to protect them from being bitten and torn during a fight.

When the cat rotates her ears towards the back and then lowers them, she is very definitely angry and probably not frightened enough to retreat (or ears would be flattened). She is very likely to attack. You might notice these ears if your cat is ready to pounce upon another cat who has pushed too far. Hopefully, no one in your household will ever be the target of such behavior. (If so, it could mean that the cat has been mistreated.)

Why do cats bite your hand during petting?

How dare she bite the hand that pets her! In her defense, your darling devil is most likely just showing good boundaries. While cats crave our undivided attention and love to be fussed over, they most definitely want it on their own terms. Unlike a dog — who never seems to get enough petting — a cat has firm, albeit fluctuating parameters for how often and how long she'll tolerate petting. Sometimes a few strokes will satisfy kitty's need for touch and at other times only a lengthy session of caresses will suffice. (Humans are actually not so different!) You'd have to be a mind reader to figure this out every time and perfectly accommodate kitty's delicate feline petting preferences, so now and then she makes it "easy" for you and nips at your hand when she's had enough. Or quite the opposite, some cats will take a pre-emptive bite as if to say, "I do hope these are not merely token strokes, and that you're not going to rush off before I've had my share." Like I said, cats know exactly how much petting they'd like and how often. They also reserve the right to change their minds several times per day.

Why do cats "knead" people with their paws?

Kneading is the very distinct trampling most cats do with their paws on the laps of their favorite people and upon soft surfaces around the house. The gentle pummeling action is used to deposit the cat's personal scent all around its territory, but what's really driving kitty to engage in this activity is pure pleasure.

Kneading, or "milk treading" as it's often referred to, is an endearing leftover from kittenhood when all the kittens would stimulate mama cat's milk flow by kneading her underside. For a kitten, these warm, snuggly moments with mama cat are total bliss and your adult cat still finds deep comfort in mimicking and possibly remembering its early nurturing. If your cat treads upon your lap often, it probably means she views you as a surrogate mother — especially if you are very quiet and relaxed, just how a mother cat would be during nursing.

You may be wondering about sharp claws digging into your skin during kneading and how you can enjoy this cozy bonding time as much as kitty! You might try only letting kitty knead when you're in thicker clothing or when you've got a blanket or throw to protect your legs.

Some cat experts discourage kneading as if the behavior fosters some immaturity in our cats, but cats really seem to love it and crave the warmth and security, so I join with many others and heartily say, why not?

Why do cats like massage?

Savvy and self-pampering, cats surely know a good thing when they see it — or feel it as the case may be. Massage is a form of therapy many humans have yet to experience but that shouldn't stop us from offering it to kitty. We all know that cats love to be petted at just the right time, for just so long and in just the proper places; the same applies to massage, or "deep petting." Cats like massage for the same reasons we like massage — it feels warm and wonderful. Massage relieves tension as muscle tissues are slowly worked and rubbed, allowing blood to flow freely and kitty to feel deliciously relaxed.

Some of kitty's favorite places are the back of neck, chest, shoulders and down the spine. (Hint: start slow; proceed gently; stop if your cat gets the least bit unsure.) Kitty will likely begin purring and she may drop into a dreamy sleep, eternally grateful for your magical, soothing touch. Some cats devour long sessions of methodical all-over massage but most cats prefer a shorter time, perhaps 5-10 minutes. Kitty may gradually increase her appetite for massage as she becomes more comfortable with it. The trick, however, is getting her to return the favor to you — now that would be something to meow about.

Why do cats' eyes change so much?

We may not always be able to determine what a cat is saying with his eyes, but we can see that a cat's eyes are ever-changing. The cat's awesome, expressive eyes are discussed here not in an attempt to positively decode them, but to playfully enjoy and explore them. This dimension of your cat's body language is highly subjective and open to all kinds of entertaining interpretation. The following descriptions are meant to prompt your own ponderings about your cat's eyes.

wide open eyes
alert? intense? interested? terrified? surprised? anxious? excited? unsure? bewildered? shocked? anticipating?

half closed eyes
studying? surveying? solving? wondering? relaxed? sleepy? content? bored? pretending to be bored? suspicious?

eyes are just showing a sliver
really relaxed? really sleepy? really bored? really suspicious?

eyes are open but repeatedly closing half way
adoring? wishing? hoping? yearning? imagining? pleading? placating? longing?

Why do cats make a funny chattering sound?

This has got to be the weirdest sound to arise from kitty. It's an oddly charming sound that cats produce when they see prey that cannot be reached because of some obstacle in the way.

You may notice this "chirp" when your cat is looking out from a favorite window at the backyard birds, wishing he could get to them. The cat opens its mouth slightly, pulls its lips back, and then opens and closes its jaws very rapidly. The noise that results is a cross between what we know of as lip smacking and teeth chattering. If kitty is going extra wild with excitement, she might add a curious vocal utterance almost like a cry that really makes the whole thing sound peculiar!

The cat isn't attempting communication, she's just frustrated that she cannot catch this critter and inflict her legendary "killing bite." She sits there and practices the skilled move instead, relegated to merely dreaming of the snack that might have been.

Why do cats make that strange grimace?

Cats sometimes do a funny thing with their mouths when they come across a delightfully complex smell. Technically known as the "flehmen response," it is a feline reaction to an exceptionally enjoyable scent. The cat is usually walking along and maybe sniffing at this and that, only to stop abruptly. The cat will lift his head slightly, ease back his upper lip, and then open his mouth just a little. Kitty holds this position for a few seconds — mesmerized and intoxicated by the smell. The opened mouth allows the special fragrance to pass through and be studied and enjoyed by what's called the Jacobsen's organ, located in the roof of the cat's mouth. It's really a smell-taste organ about ½ inch long that cats use to analyze intriguing smells in and around their territories. This must be a pleasurable activity for cats, as they are completely lost in thought and entirely captivated by the encounter. It's an experience we humans cannot enjoy and must only guess at. Could it be something like the combination of smelling a heady flower and tasting a fine wine or a multi-layered French sauce at the same time? Who knows? But it does make me a little envious of the cat.

Why do cats meow?

It's not a growl or a bark or a roar. It's not a squawk or a tweet. And it's surely not a honk or a quack! A meow is the cats melodic, passionate song of deep feeling and expression. It is poetry and it is enchanting. Defining and describing the many meows seems impossible. There are people who study cat vocal utterances very seriously and claim that they can understand much of what cats are trying to say. Consider some gleanings from the vast world of cat meows most often heard from the domestic feline. As you listen intently to your cat, you'll be charmed at the kaleidoscope of distinctive sounds. Here are a few to get you going:

"hello"
The tone in kitty's voice is upbeat, friendly, and hints of anticipation. This is a shorter meow, and often is accompanied by a loving rub or hop onto your lap. Cats use this when entering a room or greeting you at the door.

"I want something"
This meow is more like a whine and ranges in intensity from very mild to downright grating. Cats love to perfect this — they try to wear us down and make us give in! This meow is used by a lonely or hungry cat, a cat who smells raw meat, a cat who is desperately trying to lure you to play, or anytime kitty really wants something! Note where

kitty is and what she might be wanting. Some cats will walk towards the desired thing if encouraged by a willing human.

"is it okay to . . ?"

Kitty almost sounds like she's asking a question when she uses this meow; in fact that's usually just what she's doing. It's a soft, vibrating utterance that is so endearing you cannot possibly say "no" to whatever it is! Cats avail themselves of this meow when they are in a certain mellow mood and wish for a blessing for something they'd like to do. It could be a desire to come up onto your lap, to be finger fed a dot of yogurt, or to be allowed into a particular nook that's normally inaccessible. This is not a demanding meow and that could be why it's so hard to turn down.

"get closer and I'll make you wish you didn't"

Watch out for this one. It doesn't even sound nice. Kitty is unhappy with whatever it is you're doing to him or with him. This meow is more like a low-pitched war cry that is meant to warn or suffer the consequences! It can be short, or long and drawn out. Cats battling over territory will use this on each other.

"well this is very interesting . ."

This meow itself is interesting, and that makes it nearly irresistible to seek out kitty and see just what she's found. It starts out with kind of a long hum and then escalates slightly in pitch and volume with a short meow. You can almost hear the curiosity in its voice as if saying, "What have I got here?" or maybe, "Is it alive?" Kitty could have just discovered a lost toy or a meandering bug. It often has something to do with hunting or play hunting practice.

"may I, might I, pretty-please with a cherry on top?"

We're talking heart-melting with this one. Picture the cat sitting somewhere, perhaps on a chair at the dinner table. With one smooth, complete movement he meows tenderly but with his whole entire body, kind of thrusting himself softly forward as he opens his mouth and lets out a silky, muted, earnest, impassioned sound that is full of feeling, all the way from the tips of his little kitty toes. Have you witnessed this? What creature other than a cat pleads so deeply, yet so discreetly. If your cat graces your home with this meow, feel lucky. And if your kitty ever uses it on you, (as in you're the one he wants to rub or connect with and not merely the culinary delicacy at hand) then do indeed feel favored.

Why do cats purr?

Cats make the world a sweeter place just by exuding this yummy, audible vibration. Most purring, by far, is the cat's way of expressing utter contentment and joy, something like the deep, warm, sincere smile of a human. However, kitty may also use the alluring purr to get your attention, to smooth over a wrong, or to try and make you give in.

A cat may also purr when approaching another cat with whom it wants to play, not fight; it's a sign of friendliness when the cat community is out socializing. An extremely sick, defenseless cat may purr when a person or animal comes near in an effort to calm any aggression that might arise from this potential enemy. Female cats purr when they are in labor. Mother cats purr as they near their blind and deaf newborn kittens to reassure them that it's only mama cat coming near to nurse. The kittens purr back in response to signal that they are receiving their mother's milk. Scientists are not certain precisely where in the cat's body the purr originates or exactly how the body physiologically pulls it off. How fitting that the purr would be so elusive! What is known and widely accepted is that the purring sound is made from the rapid pulling apart of two vocal chords — some say "false" vocal chords because they are two membrane folds behind the actual vocal chords. Cats purr at the rate of 26 cycles per second, which explains why purring is likened to the sound of a whirring motor. The feline is the only animal in the world that purrs. Come now, are we really that surprised?

Why do cats like to sleep atop us in bed?

We are such lovable companions for our cats, and bedtime is a great opportunity for some heavy duty bonding with us! One look at a group of sleeping cats and you can see that they don't mind sleeping draped over one another, so why would we mind? It's just the feline custom to sleep in a group and cats are certainly not aware that humans may find it strange or annoying in any way. Our large, warm, uniquely-scented bodies offer security, coziness, and a whole heap of well-being for kitty, regardless of whether or not we share those particular sentiments. No matter — kitty will probably persist at lying on your head or your legs unless she eventually grows weary of getting tossed aside. Don't always be too quick to fling her away . . . she's your faithful feline friend and she just wants to stay close.

Why do cats like paper bags?

To a cat, the basic brown paper grocery bag is a crisp, fresh new toy, just waiting to be personally scent-marked, cleverly hidden within, ripped and pounced upon. Kitty views this toy as something she can use for hunting practice, which is what feline playtime is all about anyway. Cats love to pretend that they are stalking prey and a stiff brown sack works quite well for this. They can hide behind or inside it, they can move it across the floor, and then enthusiastically pounce at the trapped imaginary critter. The bag holds its shape pretty well but also scrunches and smashes to further add interest to the hunting game. Cats like things that make interesting sounds and the crinkle of paper is one of their favorites. Stick a fake mouse inside the bag or tap the outside when the cat is crouching inside to mimic the patter of little creature feet, and you'll be providing kitty with some exercise and mental stimulation. Older bags usually lose their appeal after awhile so it's best to pull out a new one often. (Avoid using bags with handles as kitty can get tangled.)

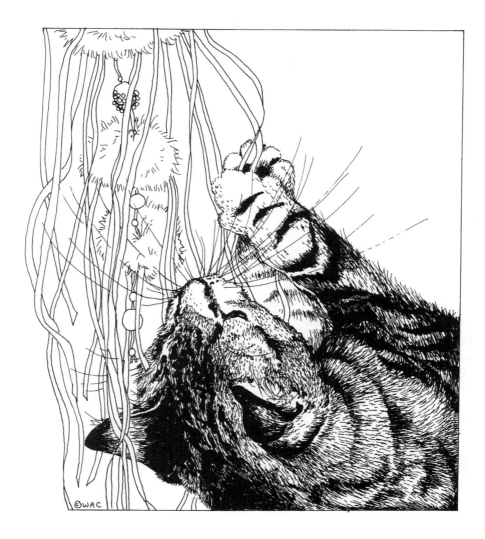

Why do cats bat at dangly things?

Cats are acutely interested in any small thing that is fast moving or any small thing that they can easily get to move fast with a flick of their deft little paws. Why? Well for one thing, it's just plain fun, but most importantly, it is a highly-prized hunting skill that cats simply love to hone. What great pleasure and satisfaction kitty feels at the ability to adeptly snatch things with consistency and precision, especially objects that happen to be bobbing, dangling, or otherwise moving around erratically. Flying things are particularly tempting and remind kitty of winged insects, birds and even fish — and their vivid imagination doesn't need a whole lot to create a rather intense game. For a cat, the tougher the challenge of capture the better — it only boosts their confidence and swells their pride. Of course, being the cheeky characters that they are, cats may not always possess the most altruistic motives for batting at stuff; at times their main objective might be attracting your attention and they know that tugging at the floating fern frond or the swinging drapery tassel will guarantee plenty!

Why do cats get stuck in trees?

It occurs at least once in the life of most every cat: kitty climbs higher and higher up into a tree and before he knows it, he's gone much farther than he'd planned. Peering down through the branches, sheer panic sets in when he realizes that it would require a long, risky jump to reach the ground. Next, kitty tries to use his claws to ease him down, but becomes acutely aware that his amazing claws are suited for climbing up a tree, not down. Cat claws are specially curved for one-direction traction and only when the cat goes backwards down a tree will the claws hook into the bark and keep him from falling. The pitiful, helpless cries of the stranded feline can be heard throughout the neighborhood and it doesn't take long for someone to follow the painful wailing sounds right to the base of a tree. With gentle, patient coaxing by a caring person most cats will figure out that they must back down the tree, and they will eventually do just that until their happy paws hit firm ground. Of course, nobody says it's easy to stand by and listen to a terrified cat try to climb down out of a tree, so get out the ladder and rescue kitty if you must, knowing that he may not learn this tree navigating skill if you resort to the quick fix.

Why do cats always land on their feet?

Well for starters, cats don't always land on their feet, but thankfully they make a safe landing nearly every time. After all, they only need 1.8 seconds to perfectly "right" themselves in the air and touch down with unbelievable grace, ease, and accuracy. In other words, even if a cat falls from a height of just one foot she technically has enough time and distance to accomplish this marvelous split-second maneuver. It all begins in the feline inner ear, where a signal is transmitted to the brain about the exact position of the cat's head in relation to the ground. Within nanoseconds, the brain orders the head to level itself and then the body follows by first twisting the upper part of the spine and then the rear half, so that at the right instant her entire body has been properly flipped into place. While all this is going on, the wondrous tail is rotating around acting as a very effective counterbalance.

Pretty cool, don't you think?

Why do cats eat grass?

The simplest answer is likely the most accurate: they like it. Cats chew and eat grass primarily because it tastes good (we like salad greens, don't we?) and they enjoy variety in their diet. Grass also happens to provide a nifty, natural vitamin B (folic acid) supplement and perhaps cats with this deficiency munch on green grass more often. Another theory is that cats nibble grass to induce vomiting up a hairball. None of these explanations contradict the other and it's fair to surmise that they're all true.

Cats do seek out the juicy clumps of green grass, so it's clear that it contains some nutrients and serves a purpose or two.

(One word of caution: houseplants are often a tempting treat for kitty but should be discouraged as there's an entire list of houseplants that are toxic to cats. However, the little pre-seeded grass pots just for cats work well.)

Why do cats cover up their half-eaten food?

This behavior is especially comical because kitty is pawing at the kitchen floor and looks rather silly as he carefully buries his food with invisible dirt! When the cat turns up his nose at mealtime and attempts to cover the food in this way, he's either protectively covering up his stash (and all trace of his scent) for a later time, or he's letting you know there's something he does not like about what's in his dish. Perhaps it's not fresh enough (cats can tell) or he's just plain bored with it and needs a little more excitement at mealtime. Offer canned tuna, a bit of cheese, or tidbit of other meat you might be fixing. Cats will usually tolerate those nutritious dry foods as long as their diet is spiced up now and then with new flavors and some good old-fashioned succulence. Also, if a cat happens to have a cold in his nose, he may forfeit eating entirely to avoid the risk of unknowingly consuming spoiled food.

Why do cats get hairballs?

Also known as "furballs," cats develop these nasty knots of swallowed fur because of their need to groom incessantly, thoroughly licking their entire furry coats with their rough, scrub brush tongues. You've seen those sausage-shaped masses on the floor or carpet and you've probably heard the painful sounds coming from a cat attempting to spit one up. It is a dreadful event, but the cat feels great relief when the hairball is finally torpedoed out of there. Small amounts of hair usually pass through the cat's system easily; but not infrequently hair builds up inside, tangles, and forms a hard, matted clump that just doesn't budge. At this point, the cat must vomit up the hairball to keep it from blocking the digestive tract, which is a potentially serious condition. (Note: tubes of "hairball remedy" are widely available in stores and their weekly use is strongly encouraged to prevent and treat hairballs.)

Cats lose bits of hair all year long, but shed heavily in the spring and fall, so then there is even more loose hair around to become ingested. Long-haired cats battle hairballs more so than the shorthairs; however, a short-hair who grooms a longhair is at greater risk too. Seems like such a grim price to pay for staying clean!

Why do cats go potty in the neighbor's garden?

If you're a gardener, this may offend you: your cat may find the neighbor's garden soil to be in better condition than your own! Cats do prefer to dig in soft, loose soil, which is why litter box training is such a snap — the several inches of litter allows them to dig easily and cover up afterwards (an instinctive practice that helps prevent predators from sensing their presence.)

In the outdoors, cats are always looking for a nice, clean, new spot in the garden to relieve themselves, and a well-nurtured flower bed is ideal. That may be part of the reason your cat visits the neighbor's garden. Another reason is to mark the outer edges of its territory with urine and feces, which is (like so much of the various marking that felines do) an attempt at claiming rights to the land. "I'm the king (or queen) here," says kitty, "I just wanted you to know that." And, of course, the marking happens over and over to keep refreshing the scent they left before or to cover up the one left previously by another cat.

Why do cats torture their prey?

Granted, it seems so cruel of kitty to slowly kill the hapless mouse, shrew, bird, bug or whatever it is she's nabbed. But the truth is, cats aren't intentionally mean and nasty. It's commonly thought that cats are purely having fun with their latest catch by prolonging the hunting game and thus, the poor critter's life. Kitty isn't aware that she is torturing the tasty, moving morsel and she certainly won't be able to comprehend your explanation nor understand your reprimand if you attempt one. Cats will do what cats will do!

Some cat experts have actually stated that they wonder if a well-fed cat (who doesn't hunt out of necessity) is even all that sure of what to do with a mouse once it's caught, so they just sit there and toy with it! However, since much of the cat's behavior is instinctive, I don't happen to agree.

Here is a thoughtful alternate possibility of what might be going on: since cats do not torture their prey every single time, could it be that the feline has flickers of mercy towards the very animal she is contemplating for her next meal? Could the cat actually be giving its prey one last fighting chance? I admit, this is a view only a true cat lover could ponder.

(Please note: The songbird population is drastically affected by house cats; as a conscientious cat owner, it may be best to leave kitty inside or tethered to a short leash.)

Why do cats bring us their latest catch?

Kitty wants to teach you how to hunt! The cat considers herself quite the skilled hunter and she considers you, well, quite the opposite. By delivering to you her latest prey, she's saying, "Hey, look what I've just caught! Wouldn't you like to learn how to hunt, too?" Your gracious response should be something like, "Oh thank you, what a good hunter you are" and "Yes, I'd like to learn but this isn't a good time." Praise the cat profusely for her sincere efforts at apprenticeship training, wait until the cat is out of sight, and then dispose of your "gift" as quickly as you can.

Seriously, cats do feel it is their responsibility to teach us humans about hunting, just as a mother cat methodically demonstrates to her kittens how to catch and eat a mouse. The process begins with mother cat bringing home a dead animal and progresses to Mama offering live prey to her kittens. Finally, the kittens join mother cat on the hunt and try it on their own. Since most adult cats are accustomed to watching their kittens participate earnestly in hunting lessons, don't be surprised if your cat looks puzzled and even disappointed when you are less than effusive about the whole thing.

Why do cats urinate on the clean laundry, the kitchen stove, in your bed and other places outside of the litter box?

A cat who urinates on the stove, on your bed, or any place that you frequent is trying desperately to get your attention for one reason or another. Either kitty is terribly unhappy with a particular aspect of daily life in the household or perhaps suffering from a painful urinary tract condition.

How do these two possibilities relate? In each case, the cat is crying for help and she knows that you will definitely (if not dramatically) notice her poor litter box habits. Cats use urine as a signal and when they deliberately go wee-wee outside of the litter box they are saying, "I'm upset. Notice me." If kitty has developed a bladder or kidney infection, she is exceedingly uncomfortable and she wants you to bring her some relief.

If no medical problem exists, the cat is acting out because of some unpleasant change or ongoing dynamic in the house. Kitty may be miffed because you are leaving her alone more than usual or because you don't have as much time for her, or because she is jealous of a new person in your life, or worse yet, because she is somehow being mistreated.

For a cat to urinate outside the litter box he or she has to be feeling mighty low or exasperated. Check with the vet for medical help. Then sit down and contemplate how the cat might be viewing and experiencing life. With extra attention, regular playtime, and loads of reassurance from kitty's favorite people, the cat will likely have no need for delinquent episodes and will resume her customary litter box etiquette.

Why do cats spend so much time licking and grooming themselves?

Cats devote nearly a third of their day to careful grooming, so I think we can safely say they are obsessed! Sometimes it indeed seems like overkill and we wonder just how dirty is this cat?

Of course, what kitty isn't telling you is that there are several perfectly good reasons for her fastidiousness besides a penchant for keeping clean. The earnest licking not only cleans and deodorizes kitty's coat, but also removes loose hair and skin, increases her blood flow, and tones her muscles. Think of it as part of kitty's daily workout routine.

Some cats also groom themselves when they are uncertain how to behave in a certain social situation or when they are unusually nervous — merely sitting there looking awkward would never do for a dignified feline!

Cats may also lick their coats to regulate body temperature. In the cold, repeated licking smoothes down the fur and acts as an insulating layer. On hot days, kitty may lick her fur to feel the cooling effects of evaporation, much as we benefit from the evaporation of sweat on our skin. And when it's raining, there's some automatic waterproofing going on — the licking stimulates glands in the skin that secrete a natural protective substance.

Why do cats hiss?

They are mimicking snakes! It's true — cats and most other animals are dreadfully afraid of snakes and cats have chosen to imitate the deadly snake in order to terrorize another cat, a dog, other enemy, or even a person who appears hostile. A cat begins by flattening its ears and widening its jaw, thus taking on a snake-like appearance. You might see the tail swooshing back and forth too, which further suggests the movements of a snake. The actual hissing occurs when the cat opens her mouth part way, pulls back her upper lip, and forcefully releases her breath. Sometimes moisture accompanies the paralyzing hissing sound and then you get what is known as spitting. To be sure, hissing is an effective warning from kitty that seems to communicate in no uncertain terms that she is a force to be reckoned with. (Please note: be careful not to mimic the hiss in an attempt to stop your cat from doing something; you will cause her to be afraid of you and then you will become an enemy in her eyes instead of an ally or friend.)

Why do cats arch their backs?

A cat with an arched back is in a fearful, defensive mode and he's trying to make himself look larger and more threatening. Cats are able to arch their backs so high because their spines contain nearly 60 vertebrae, twice what we have. They demonstrate this incredible flexibility when trying to intimidate each other. Often kitty will turn sideways to display an even more impressive profile, or his coat will fluff up as well, thus the descriptive phrase, "its hair was standing up on end." This adds to the heightened and fearsome look. What's happening is that certain hairs are responding to an adrenaline rush. When kitty feels superior, it's just the hair along the spine that sticks up. If kitty perceives he may not be in the stronger position during an encounter, his entire coat may stand up. These are great looks for cartoons, but probably not what we want to see very often from our own little darlin's.

Why do cats sound as if they're killing each other when mating?

To be sure, the curious mating rituals of the feline produce endless fascination on the part of onlookers. It's a wonder that cats mate at all, considering the pain and anguish that appear to characterize the sexual encounter. The operative word here could be "appears" as it's just not all that certain why the female cat emits her infamous blood-curdling scream during the 10-second copulation. It has long been thought that the female cat experienced terrible pain, not as the male cat penetrated but upon exit, as the "spines" on his penis scraped her vagina. This theory has weakened however, since scientists have experimented with inserting a smooth, glass rod and the female cats scream just as loud. Could this sharp cry actually be a strange pleasurable scream? Is kitty experiencing orgasmic rapture or is she merely at wits end by the stress of being in estrus ("in heat") and simply ready to be over and done with it? After all, she has writhed on the ground in some kind of sexual misery, she has fought off unsuitable male after unsuitable male, and she's been restrained by her "lover" with a bite on the scruff of her neck just before mounting. Hmmm . . . we can only hope that what we are hearing is ecstasy and not agony.

Why do cats dash madly around the house?

Relax, they don't do this to drive you crazy. Flying around at speeds of up to 30 miles per hour, cats who tear around the house with no apparent stimuli are merely burning off vast quantities of stored energy. This is perfectly normal feline behavior, especially for a mostly indoor cat who doesn't get enough exercise. Being nocturnal animals, the house will usually turn into a racetrack at night when cats would naturally hunt.

In the wild, cats sleep by day to store up the energy to chase and kill by night. For house cats, a meal is hand delivered and it is not incumbent upon kitty to fetch for himself. The instinct to run and chase and catch prey is still very much alive and well, however.

So if you're awakened by your cat's late-night antics, try to remember that this is an indication that kitty is actually quite sane and healthy, albeit a little under exercised. Roll over, go back to sleep, wait until the light of day . . . and tomorrow you can learn to play indoor soccer with your cat.

Why do cats like catnip?

Well, there's just no sophisticated way to say this: cats like catnip because it gives them a "high." Catnip is really a drug for kitties. I'm not speaking of the same kind of drug habit that humans experience, though — catnip is generally considered quite safe. And it's not as if the cat frantically seeks out the catnip in order to achieve an altered state. If the catnip is around, then fine. If not, that seems to be all right, too.

There are two main theories as to how catnip affects cats; one is that it contains an odor similar to something in cat urine and the other is that the chemical nepetalactone, an unsaturated lactone found in catnip, acts as a drug.

Whichever it is, most cats usually take a brief drug trip from sniffing it, chewing it, and finally rolling in it — quite a frolicking frenzy to behold. Some say that prolonged indulgence may lead to personality changes in a small percentage of cats, but the vast majority of kitties are able to enjoy the 10 minutes of euphoria that catnip provides without any negative side effects.

Why do cats seem so aloof?

Most standoffish cats didn't start out that way. Some-where along the line, cats like this were repeatedly mishandled, excluded, ignored or frightened by humans who just didn't understand the feline psyche. Often accused of being haughty, cold and disdainful, the cat has really had to work diligently at shaking this poor reputation. Cats are sensitive, responsive creatures who usually require humans to take the initiative when it comes to affection and involvement.

Of course, there are exceptions, but generally speaking, the cat looks to us to set the household standard for closeness and "together time." If we don't go out of our way to deliberately invite kitty into our everyday lives, kitty will keep her distance. If we don't bother to shower kitty with affection, she will reciprocate. And so on (I think you get the idea).

But here's the good news: once a cat is heartily welcomed into the family, you are granted the privilege of watching her blossom and develop into a tender, lov-ing feline! Of course, cats aren't going to respond with the same effervescence and energy of dogs, but within the context of feline expression, it's safe to predict that you will be thoroughly charmed and thrilled by your cat's warm acceptance of you and her sincere desire to be in your midst. Given the opportu-nity, most cats will gladly come close — and the word "aloof" slips entirely from one's vocabulary.

Why do cats refuse to cooperate?

The short answer is that cats are more like humans and less like dogs. We are accustomed to the joy that a dog exhibits when his master calls and he comes, or when he's told to sit and he sits, or when he faithfully returns with the Frisbee, and so on. Sure, dogs need some training and on-going positive reinforcement, but by and large, the canine is a pack animal who is hard wired to accept and genuinely like following orders.

Not so the cat! The independent feline enjoys following orders about as much as we do. Cats will cooperate with people and other cats, but there has definitely got to be something in it for them. Kitty is perfectly willing to arrive at your side when called or hop down from that sensational napping spot when you ask him to, if he believes that something worthwhile will present itself when he does. The obvious rewards are tuna, milk, other special food treats, catnip, or a favorite toy or game. Less obvious rewards are things you do with and for the cat such as attentively petting him, greeting him warmly, or inviting him onto your lap.

Cats usually won't lift a paw to cooperate for cooperation's sake . . . but you'd be surprised what they'll do in the name of friendship.

Why do cats interrupt our phone conversations?

When we talk on the phone, we often speak in a soft, lyrical voice, and guess what? Kitty thinks we are talking to her! No wonder she jumps up and down from our lap and cannot seem to stay away when we are jabbering into the telephone — she has no clue that we are conversing with someone in the little gadget we hold to our ear.

To the cat, our animated chatter can be irresistible and our sedentary lap an open invitation. Sometimes our vocalizations may coincide with how we're looking at her or petting her while talking into the phone, but for the most part kitty is quite confused if we seem to be speaking to her but not petting her.

So don't push the cat away next time . . . whisper her name, stroke her, and be thankful for a few moments of built-in bonding time.

Why do cats sit down on what we are reading?

There are a few humorous theories to explain this phenomenon and I love them all. The first purports that the cat insists on being right in the middle of things, lathered with our full attention in a precocious, whenever-I-please-thank-you-very-much sort of way. Once you've lived with a cat, this explanation is very easy to believe.

It could also be true, however, that kitty isn't as overly confident as she seems, and her desire to have top billing every night is actually a sincere quest for reassurance that she is as incredibly adored as she was last night. The longer I know cats, the more I think this is true in many instances.

A third explanation for this forward, in-your-face kind of presence is possibly the sweetest of all: perhaps kitty notices that you are oh so busy and takes it upon herself to give you a little break from your work. Hmmm, the more I think about that one, the more I think kitty is pulling our leg, but it sure makes a nice story.

Why do cats completely endear themselves to us?

Now this is a mystery, for cats are so very capable of living life solo. They don't really need us, yet they like us, really. They desire our companionship — they want to be a member of the family.

They aren't known for making many promises, but they surely aren't the self-centered creatures they are often made out to be, either. Cats could so easily run away and have a perfectly interest-ing and satisfying life far away from humans, and in some ways it might be more efficient or feline-friendly: no loud music coming through speakers, no commotion during the day when they are trying to sleep, no wondering whether or not the food will truly arrive in the bowl.

Without us, there would be no limit of things to scale or climb, no break-ables to dodge, no silly rules or strange customs. Yes, we do provide goodies and warmth and our cats know they've got it good, but it's far more than that. Don't underestimate the cat's capacity for love! The cat chooses friendship with humans and grants us entrance into their world — and in the process we become mesmerized by them.

We find that we will do almost any-thing for these creatures because they have become our friends and also because they are beautiful . . . and we enjoy this living, pulsating work of art right in our midst. The show is ever-changing, yet comfortingly the same. We are so lucky that this soft, silky, independent piece of wildness steps daily into our homes and announces through ears, tail, eyes, purrs, meows, body, and all else feline, that he is utterly content and that he wouldn't have life any other way. Well, that is, until tomorrow morning at 6 AM. And you've just got to love that, too.

KAREN ANDERSON

is also the author of

Cats Have No Masters . . . Just Friends

and

The Cat-Sitter's Handbook: A Personalized Guide
for Your Pet's Caregiver

also published by Willow Creek Press